Made in the USA
Monee, IL
04 November 2019

16295438R00030

GOLF CLUBS FOR BEGINNERS

A Beginner's Guide to
Understanding Golf Clubs and
How to Use Them

Text Copyright © Lightbulb Publishing

All rights reserved. No part of this guide may be reproduced in any form without permission in writing from the publisher except in the case of brief quotations embodied in critical articles or reviews.

Legal & Disclaimer

The information contained in this book and its contents is not designed to replace or take the place of any form of medical or professional advice; and is not meant to replace the need for independent medical, financial, legal or other professional advice or services, as may be required. The content and information in this book has been provided for educational and entertainment purposes only.

The content and information contained in this book has been compiled from sources deemed reliable, and it is accurate to the best of the Author's knowledge, information, and belief. However, the Author cannot guarantee its accuracy and validity and cannot be held liable for any errors and/or omissions. Further, changes are periodically made to this book as and when needed. Where appropriate and/or necessary, you must consult a professional (including but not limited to your doctor, attorney, financial advisor or such other professional advisor) before using any of the suggested remedies, techniques, or information in this book.

Upon using the contents and information contained in this book, you agree to hold harmless the Author from and against any damages, costs, and expenses, including any legal fees potentially resulting from the application of any of the information provided by this book. This disclaimer applies to any loss, damages or injury caused by the use and application, whether directly or indirectly, of any advice or information presented, whether for breach of contract, tort, negligence, personal injury, criminal intent, or under any other cause of action.

You agree to accept all risks of using the information presented in this book.

You agree that by continuing to read this book, where appropriate and/or necessary, you shall consult a professional (including but not limited to your doctor, attorney, or financial advisor or such other advisor as needed) before using any of the suggested remedies, techniques, or information in this book.

Table of Contents

Chapter One
Introduction

For a beginner, golf can be a little intimidating. Okay, let's be honest – for a beginner, golf can be really intimidating. There are new terms to learn, complicated techniques to master, friends to make, and much more. It's easy to be overwhelmed when you are new to this game, and you might be tempted to simply turn around and walk away. We don't want that to happen, however, as golf is a game which can provide you with great experiences and incredible memories – as long as you stick it out long enough to get past the initial learning curve.

In this guide, we are going to address one of the issues that give many new golfers trouble – picking out a set of clubs. How do you know what to look for? How do you know how much to spend? There are many questions to answer before you can build your first set properly, and you might not have anyone available to answer those questions for you. With this guide, we aim to offer the answers you need to make smart decisions right from the start.

Why This Matters

First things first, we need to explain why it is important to pick out the right set of clubs as a beginning golfer. Some beginners make the mistake of thinking that their low skill level means they don't need to worry about which clubs they use.

Nothing could be further from the truth. While you don't necessarily need to invest in a high-end set of clubs that costs thousands of dollars, you shouldn't settle for just using the first set you can get your hands on. By taking some time to locate a set that makes sense for your needs, you will be getting your golf experience off to a great start.

As you are soon to find out, golf is an extremely difficult game. Most would agree it is one of the most difficult games in the world. If you were to play with a set of clubs that did not fit your skills, you would be taking a game that is already hard and making it even harder. That is not something you want to do, of course. You have enough work in front of you anyway just learning this game, don't add another speed bump by failing to do your homework with regard to equipment.

Building a Set

Before you go shopping, it's important to know what you'll need to buy in order to assemble a proper set of clubs. Under the Rules of Golf, you are allowed to carry 14 clubs in your bag for any given round. So, looking for 14 clubs is a great place to start. Some advanced players will own more than this, so they can pick and choose which ones they are going to use on a day to day basis, but you don't need to worry about that now. Start with a set of 14 and go from there.

While 14 clubs might seem like a lot to a beginner, you will quickly learn that you will need each and every one of them. Sure,

you probably won't use all of them in each round, but you will use them often enough to warrant keeping each of them in your set. It is up to you to decide which clubs will make up your set, but there are many choices that you'll want to be sure to include. The list below is a great place to get started –

- Driver

- Three wood

- Five wood

- Five irons (five iron through nine iron)

- Three wedges

- Putter

The list above adds up to 12 clubs in total. That leaves two more spots available for you to fill. You may decide to add another fairway wood, such as a seven wood, or you might opt for a hybrid club or two. Some golfers will add a fourth wedge in order to provide themselves with more options in the short game and on short approach shots. We will get into this topic in greater detail later in the guide, but you should now have a basic idea of how to construct a useful set of clubs.

Using This Guide

In the guide that follows, we are going to provide you with some pieces of information that you can use to direct your

shopping process. Please take a bit of time to read through the advice below and consider taking notes in order to remember the important points. Shopping for golf clubs is not the most complicated thing you'll do in your life, but that doesn't mean you should take it for granted. Educate yourself, make a plan, and head out to find the perfect set.

With that said, let's not wait any longer to get started!

Chapter Two
Drivers

For many golfers, the driver is the most exciting club in the bag. As it is the club that will hit the ball the farthest – when used correctly, of course – it is easy to understand why so many golfers enjoy pulling their driver out of the bag on the tee of the par fours and par fives. To get the best possible performance out of your driver, you'll want to make sure to buy one that fits your swing perfectly.

In this chapter, we are going to go over some of the key points you need to keep in mind while looking for a driver. If you walk into a local golf shop or even browse on a golf equipment website, you'll find that there are an incredible number of drivers available today. And, many of them sell for hundreds of dollars, so we are talking about a big buying decision. Take some time to pick up some basic knowledge with regard to drivers and you'll be much better prepared to make a smart choice.

The Modern Game

One of the first things new golfers will notice when shopping for a driver is the sheer size of golf driver heads. If you maybe played a bit of golf many years ago, only to go away from the game, it might be shocking to see just how much the clubs have grown. Driver club heads a couple decades ago were relatively moderate in size compared to the clubs of today. These days, most driver clubheads are 460cc in volume, which is the limit allowed under the rules of golf. You'll occasionally see options

that are slightly smaller than this maximum size, but most of the options on the market do hit the 460cc mark.

As a beginner, it is a good idea to select one of these 460cc drivers. Using the largest possible clubhead allowed under the rules is going to provide you a few advantages, as described below.

- Forgiveness. The big advantage to be gained when using a large-headed driver is the forgiveness offered by the sheer size of the club head. There is plenty of room on the face for you to make contact, even if you do miss the sweet spot by a bit. If you were to use a smaller driver head, perhaps by finding an older model club for sale online somewhere (or at a garage sale), you would be missing out on some of that forgiveness. You shouldn't expect your swing to be particularly consistent when first getting started in golf, so making contact on the sweet spot with regularity is going to be unlikely. Pick out a driver with a 460cc head so you can give yourself as much room to work with at impact as possible.

- Distance. Often, drivers with a large volume are going to provide you with a bit more distance than smaller clubs. The face of such a driver should have plenty of 'spring' to offer, as long as the club is relatively new (and of good quality). The size of the club head is certainly not the only factor when it comes to how far your shots are going to travel, but it's a piece of the puzzle.

- Confidence. There is something about looking down at your driver at address and seeing a big club head that is going to

boost your confidence a bit. As a new golfer, you are going to need all the confidence you can muster, as this is a game which tends to punish those who are just getting started. Specifically, it's important to feel confident on your tee shots, as you need to put the ball in play off the tee as often as you can. It's likely that you won't feel particularly confident with most of your clubs as you work on learning the game, so feeling relatively confident with the driver is one big step in the right direction.

So, the first point you are going to look for in a driver is a 460cc head. With that on your shopping list, the next thing to think about is the shaft of the club. Even experienced golfers tend to make the mistake of overlooking the important role that the shaft plays within any golf club – and especially the driver. You can think of the shaft as the engine of the driver. Yes, the club head is important, as we stated above, but the shaft of the club really needs to match up with the dynamics of your swing appropriately.

For a beginner, picking out the right club shaft can be a bit tricky. While the best way to dial in the right shaft for your game is to go through a club fitting process with a professional, that might not be something you are ready to do just yet. So, what do you do about picking the right shaft as a beginner? The key is to err on the softer side for now. Golf club shafts tend to come with designations of 'regular', 'stiff', or 'extra stiff'. Players with lower swing speeds need to remain in the 'regular' category, while players who swing harder will want to look at 'stiff' or 'extra stiff' models.

Err on the Soft Side

For the typical beginning male golfer, a 'regular' flex is going to be the right choice. You probably won't have huge swing speed when first getting started, so opting for a regular flex club makes a lot of sense. You can always move into a stiffer model later on as your swing improves and your power increases. Starting out with a shaft that is too stiff for the dynamics of your swing is going to make it very hard to get the ball up off the ground – and that experience will be quite frustrating. Most beginners will be best-served to start with a 'regular' flex and move on from there.

It should be noted that senior golfers may be a good fit for a 'senior' flex shaft, and women will often be well-suited for a 'ladies' flex (as the names would indicate). Of course, there is plenty of variation among individuals within those groups, so not every senior or woman is going to be a good match for a 'senior' or 'ladies' flex. However, as a beginner in one of those categories, that is a good place to start.

Before we finish up this chapter on drivers, we do need to mention that it is absolutely not necessary to spend top dollar when buying your first driver. Many of the new drivers on the market from the top brands will cost somewhere between $400 - $500 for just the one club – and that is not a price you need to pay as a beginning player. You don't yet know how much you will like this game, or how often you will be able to play. It simply wouldn't make sense to invest such a large amount of money in one club. Those expensive clubs aren't going anywhere, and you can always buy one later if you decide the cost is worth it to you.

Later in this guide, we'll get into the topic of how to find the right clubs while remaining within a reasonable budget.

Chapter Three
Irons

It might feel like you had to spend a lot of time picking out a driver, just to fill one single spot in your bag, you'll get a little more return on your time investment when shopping for irons. You'll still want to take your time and make a smart choice, of course, but irons are sold in sets rather than as individual clubs. Depending on the set you purchase, you will be able to fill six, seven, or even eight spots in your bag all at once.

As was the case with drivers, there many options to consider in the irons market. The first thing you are going to want to watch for is the style of the club head used in a given iron set. There are two main categories of iron heads – blades and cavity backs. On this point, we can make things pretty simple for you. As a beginning golfer, you will want to purchase a set of cavity back irons. While blade irons can certainly look pretty, and they are a great option for a more experienced player, you are not yet to that point in your golf journey. You may find that a set of blades is a good pick for you at some point in the future, but it is best to start off with a cavity back set and go from there.

What's the Difference?

At this point, we should probably back up a little bit and explain the difference between cavity back and blade irons. As the name would indicate, a cavity back iron is one with a cavity in the back of the club head. The bulk of the club head is found

around the perimeter, while there is very little material in the center of the club. These clubs are also referred to as 'perimeter-weighted' irons because the majority of the weight of the club head is found around the edges.

By contrast, blade irons are a similar thickness from the toe to the heel. It's a much simpler design, and many golfers find these kinds of clubs to be more visually attractive than cavity backs. While that may be the case, they are not a good choice for beginners because of the limited forgiveness they offer. A shot struck on the sweet spot with a blade iron will feel great – but even a slightly miss-hit is going to be a problem. The shot will feel terrible coming off the club and it will likely wind up short of the target. You need to be an accomplished golfer with a refined swing technique in order to use blades effectively.

The reason cavity back irons are so useful for beginning players is the forgiveness they offer on miss-hits. They are the complete opposite of blade irons in this way. Rather than punishing you for missing the sweet spot, cavity backs will do their best to help your ball still reach the target. You'll still want to hit the ball with the sweet spot as often as possible, of course, but you'll 'get away' with your misses a bit more when holding a cavity back iron.

They Aren't Perfect

Before moving on to the other keys that you should keep in mind when iron shopping, we do want to stop for a moment and talk about the drawbacks to using cavity back irons. While we do

think they are the best option for beginners, they are by no means perfect golf clubs, and you may get to a point in your golf journey when they are no longer the best option for your game. The list below touches on three key drawbacks you may experience in the future if you stick with cavity backs.

- Difficulty with distance control. This is perhaps the biggest complaint with regard to perimeter-weighted clubs. It can be tough to control the distance of your shots precisely, especially with short irons. Say, for example, that you want to hit a 110-yard approach shot, but your nine iron usually hits the ball 120-yards (and your PW can't quite reach all the way to 110). If you choke up on the club and make a softer swing in an effort to take distance off the shot, you may find that the ball still flies the same distance. With a blade iron, you are more likely to have the ability to manipulate your distances by a few yards when necessary. This is an advanced skill, and nothing you should worry about now, but it may come into play down the line.

- Inability to hit low shots. Most beginning golfers spend a lot of time working on getting the ball up off the ground. At first, it can seem like an impossible task to hit the ball more than a few feet off the ground. As you continue to grow as a golfer, however, you'll find that there are actually some occasions where you'll want to hit those lower shots. For example, when the wind is blowing, hitting a low ball is a great way to limit the impact of the wind on your shots. Unfortunately, it is difficult to hit low shots with cavity back irons, as they are

specifically designed to help the player get the ball up into the air. You'll love that benefit when first getting started, but it could become frustrating at some point, especially if you develop your skills to an advanced level.

- Limited ability to hit curves. As a new golfer, hitting a shot that curves is usually what you are trying to avoid. Beginning golfers are typically trying to hit the ball as straight as possible, and that is understandable. As you gain experience, you'll find that you actually want to use those curves to your advantage from time to time. You may want to hit a draw to get around a tree, or you may want to hit a fade in order to reach a hole located on the right side of the green. Whatever the case, advanced golfers value the ability to curve the ball on command. With a cavity back club, you are always going to struggle to do just that. These clubs are built with the idea of hitting the ball as straight as possible, meaning subtle shot shaping can be a challenge.

We need to state again here that these points are not for you to worry about now. As a beginner, you can ignore the three points above and move forward with a set of cavity back irons. Keep them in the back of your mind and pay attention to how your performance develops over time. If it turns out that you seem to have a knack for this game, and you start to shoot quality scores after a while, you may need to switch away from perimeter weighted irons.

It should be clear at this point that cavity back irons are the right pick for beginners. But what else should you be looking for in an iron set? Let's work through a quick list of other points to watch for while you shop.

- Type of shaft. There are two options here – graphite shafts and steel shafts. Unfortunately, there isn't a right answer that can be applied across the board. Steel shafts will work just fine for many new golfers, and that option tends to be more affordable than graphite. With that said, opting for graphite will usually provide you with a club that weighs less overall, meaning you might be able to swing a graphite-shafted club faster than a club with a steel shaft. Many senior golfers do find that graphite is a better fit than steel, so keep that in mind if you are getting started in this game in your later years.

- Number of clubs. One of the biggest decisions you'll need to make is simply settling on how many clubs you would like to have in your iron set. Generally speaking, the shortest club in an iron set is going to be the pitching wedge, and you will work up from there. It used to be that a traditional iron set would include eight clubs, but times are changing, and few golfers actually carry that many irons anymore. A full set of eight irons would take you all the way up to a three iron, and it's quite unlikely you'll be able to hit quality shots with a three iron as a beginner (many golfers never reach the point of hitting good shots with the long irons). We would recommend, as a beginner, that you stop at the five iron when picking out an iron set. That means you'll have just six irons

in your set, and you'll have plenty of room in your bag for additional fairway woods or hybrids. Remember, the goal here is to make the game as easy as possible at first, and this decision will serve that purpose. If you would like to try long irons later on as your skills improve, there will always be other clubs you can buy.

- Look of the club. This last point can be a bit tricky for a beginner, as you don't yet have a personal preference with regard to how clubs look. Even still, if you get the chance to look at clubs in person while shopping – or even if you are just shopping online – allow your own personal opinion of the club's appearance to play a role in your choice. You need to feel good about the shot you are preparing to hit each time you look down at an iron, so you don't want to be uncomfortable with the way the club looks.

Much like buying a driver, it is likely going to take some time to pick out a set of irons that can get you started the right way in this game. Take some time, do your research to learn about various brands and the prices that come with them, and only make your purchase when you are confident that you've found a good option.

Chapter Four
Wedges

As a new golfer, it is easy to overlook the importance of the wedges. These clubs often fail to get the attention they deserve, as new golfers tend to think about the driver first and foremost, as well as the putter. You are going to be playing a lot of shots with your wedges as a beginner, however, so you'll want to make sure that an appropriate assortment is present in your set right from the start.

You'll be happy to learn that shopping for wedges might be the easiest category to fill out in your bag. There simply isn't that much variation from wedge to wedge, so you don't need to worry about the details too much. The general shape of a wedge club head is going to be similar from brand to brand and model to model. Also, you don't need to worry much about cavity back vs. blade here, since you aren't hitting particularly long shots with your wedges. If you can find wedges that you like which come with a reasonable price tag, you are pretty much ready to go.

A Cohesive Unit

So, why do we even need to dedicate a chapter in our guide to wedges if they are so easy to buy? The main point we want to make here relates to building a cohesive set of wedges that fit in nicely with one another. Remember, you are trying to build a set of clubs that will help you get around the course as effectively as possible. You only have 14 spots to work within your bag, so you

don't want to use up two of those spots with clubs that basically do the same thing. Each club should have its own purpose if you are going to get the maximum possible performance out of your set.

As we mentioned earlier, the pitching wedge is going to be the shortest iron in your set. So, from there, you are going to add either two or three more wedges which will be even shorter than the PW. The biggest thing to keep in mind on this point is the distance gapping between your wedges. Most likely, the pitching wedge in your set is going to have 46* - 48* of loft. Starting from that point, you are going to add on two or three more wedges with more loft, in order to deal with shorter shots effectively.

For example, if you decide to go with two wedges, it would be common to pick out a 52* and 58* wedge to add to your set. When paired up with your pitching wedge, that will give you a nice spread across the board and allow you to cover a number of short distances. If you hit your pitching wedge 100 yards, you may hit the 52* around 90 yards, and the 58* wedge around 75 yards. That means you'll have nice gaps between each wedge, and each club will have its own job to do.

Should you decide to go with three additional wedges, you may want to opt for a 52*, 56*, 60* setup. That is obviously going to provide you with even tighter distance gaps, although you will need to use up an additional spot in your set to go this way. It's probably sufficient to start with just two additional

wedges as you get started in golf, and you can always alter this setup later on down the line.

Watch for Wear

One more note we would like to make regarding wedges has to do with the fact that you need to replace them more frequently than perhaps any other clubs in your bag. You'll be hitting a lot of shots with your wedges, whether those shots are full swings or chip and pitches from around the green. As you use these clubs, the grooves on the face will wear out and the clubs will gradually become less effective. So, it is a good idea to watch the condition of your wedges and replace them before they are too far worn down to do their job. If you play and practice golf frequently, you might only get a single season out of your wedges. Those who play and practice less frequently should get at least a couple seasons, if not more.

Chapter Five
Putter

Believe it or not, the putter is one of the most important clubs in the bag. Many new golfers make the mistake of thinking that the putter couldn't be too important since it just rolls the ball along the ground. While it might not produce the exciting, impressive shots that a driver can create, having the right putter in your bag is essential. With a good putter in your hands, and with the right technique in place, you can quickly lower your scores.

More than any other category we are going to cover in this article, the putter is a matter of personal preference. You don't need to think at all about the technical aspects of the design of the putter, or anything like that. Sure, you could get into the details of how each putter is meant to work and what advantages it might provide, that stuff simply isn't necessary right now. The best way to proceed is to pick out a putter that you like and get started learning how to use it effectively.

Two Items to Check

While the final decision is going to come down to personal preference above all else, there are a couple points you can think about if you are so inclined. The first is the length of the putter shaft. 35" is a standard length for a putter, but you'll find models which are both longer and shorter than that number available on store shelves. How do you know which length is best for you?

Simple – try out a few options and see which one feels the best. You don't want to just base it on your height, as that really isn't going to tell you much about the putter that is going to feel best in your hands. Some short golfers like using a full 35" putter, while some taller players like using a 33" or 34" model. The best thing you can do here is to head to a local golf shop and see which length seems to suit you best.

The other point we will highlight here is the putter head style options. There are two basic categories of putter heads – mallets and blades. Unlike when we were talking about irons, where beginning golfers will want to stay away from blades, there is no such warning here. If you like the look of a blade putter head, go for it. Or, if you prefer the way a mallet looks, that is perfectly fine as well. You'll see both of these kinds of putters used at the highest levels of the game, which should be proof enough that both blades and mallets can get the job done. Start out with the model that seems to suit you well and get down to the business of learning how to putt. It will be easy enough to make a switch later if you decide that the putter you purchased is not actually a great fit for your game.

Chapter Six
Hybrids

The last category of clubs we are going to cover is hybrids. You might not know it if you are just getting started in the world of golf, but hybrid clubs are actually quite new to this game themselves. They've been around in various forms for quite some time but have only really established themselves as a mainstream club option over the last 10 – 20 years. Compared to the centuries-long history of this game, that's a pretty short history.

So, why have hybrids gotten so popular in recent years? Simple – they offer a more forgiving option as compared to the long irons that so many people struggle to hit. For much of the history of the game, amateur golfers would carry long irons like the three iron and the four iron, even though they weren't really capable of hitting good shots with those clubs. It takes both ample swing speed and plenty of skill to hit good shots with long irons. The average golfer doesn't have enough of either of those things, so the long irons tended to stay in the bag. With the advent of the hybrid, golfers have been ditching their long irons in mass numbers and tossing a hybrid or two in the bag instead.

Filling a Gap

As the name would indicate, a hybrid golf club is a blend of a fairway wood and an iron. The profile of the club head tends to be thinner than that of a fairway wood, but it is thicker than a

long iron. The big gain when switching from a long iron to a hybrid is the improved weight distribution and forgiveness. Hybrids tend to have their weight gathered mostly in the sole of the club, something which is possible thanks to the hollow-head design. That means the club has a low center of gravity, and the ball should get up in the air rather easily when all is said and done.

Although hybrid clubs are a good choice for golfers of all skill levels, they are particularly important for beginners. As a beginning golfer, it's likely that you'll have quite a bit of trouble with the longer shots that you encounter on the course. When you need to hit the ball 175 yards or more, you will need to produce your best swing to get the job done. If you are holding a four iron while trying to hit such a shot, you'll be facing an uphill battle. Using a hybrid instead will give you a much better chance at success, and you will probably have more fun as a result. Hybrids are also good clubs to use off the tee when the driver just doesn't seem to be cooperating. Given their ease-of-use and the helpful role they play within a set of clubs, it makes a lot of sense for a beginning golfer to carry at least one hybrid, if not two.

When shopping for hybrids, you will find that many of them look quite similar to one another. This is good news for you as a shopper, because you aren't going to have to do as much homework in order to make a good decision. As long as you pick a club with a shaft that has an appropriate flex – you can use

what you learned when shopping for a driver to find the right shaft here as well – you should be good to go. It's possible that you could make this decision based on nothing more than brand loyalty and familiarity. If you've already purchased a driver that you like, it's almost certain that the company which made the driver also offers some hybrid clubs. Once you have acquired your hybrids to slot in between your driver/fairway woods and your irons, you may have completed your set.

Chapter Seven
Purchasing the Right Clubs

With all of the various club categories covered, let's take a step back and talk from a big-picture perspective about the task of buying golf clubs. Golf has a reputation for being an expensive game, and that reputation has certainly been well-earned over the years. Not only can be it costly to buy clubs, but it can also be expensive to pay greens fees, purchase golf balls and other accessories, buy shoes, etc. You get the picture – golf is not exactly a game for those who want to spend their recreation time on a shoestring budget.

With that said, you don't have to break the bank in order to come away with some nice golf equipment to get you started. It's simply not necessary to spend $2,000+ on your first set of clubs. Could you? Of course – that would be no problem at all. It isn't really going to help you play any better, however, and it isn't going to make the game any more fun. Basically, your goal as a new golfer should be to get started with as little money as possible while still getting the equipment you need to learn the game. The expensive clubs on the market aren't going anywhere, and you can always buy them later if you so choose.

What's Your Budget?

To get started purchasing the equipment you need, it is a good idea to set an overall budget. Of course, we don't know your personal financial situation, so we can't tell you exactly how

much you should spend. As is the case with any other purchasing decision, you should only spend what you feel comfortable with given the other aspects of your financial life. Even if you are completely committed to learning how to play golf, your newfound golf habit shouldn't get in the way of things like the mortgage or your grocery bill. Be smart so you can have fun on the course without worrying about how much money you blew through while buying your clubs and other gear.

We have touched on this topic a bit earlier in the guide, but it is worth pointing out again that you are going to have a relatively low skill level when first getting started in golf. That's not an insult – everyone starts from the bottom in this game. Even if you are an athletic person and have excelled in other sports over the years, you are almost certainly going to struggle for a period of time as you learn this difficult game. Some people will progress faster than others, of course, but everyone starts off with a rough swing and an ugly short game.

What does that have to do with equipment? Simple – you shouldn't be buying clubs that are aimed at higher level players than yourself. When you walk into a golf shop to look for clubs, the sales staff may try to sell you on the highest priced items in the store. That makes sense for them, of course, but it doesn't make any sense for you. Don't be pressured into a buying decision that you know isn't the right one at this time. Embrace your status as a beginner and pick out equipment that is meant to make the game as easy as possible for those just getting started.

Speaking of the local golf shop, we need to talk for a minute about where you should be looking to buy your clubs. Do you want to buy them online, or are you going to visit a physical store? There are pros and cons to each option, of course. Let's take a closer look at this topic.

- Online = easy. This is why online shopping is so popular in the first place, right? You can relax on your couch, browsing sites on your phone or your laptop. There are plenty of great golf retailers on the web today, so it will take only moments to track down tons of club options. When you have decided on the clubs you are going to order, you just press a couple buttons and wait for them to arrive a few days later. It certainly is a great experience and one which many new golfers will use due to convenience alone.

- Physical store offers immediate feedback. When you buy online, the club won't actually be in your hands until you receive the shipment. That means you won't be able to get a perfect impression of what the club is like until you've already purchased it. This isn't necessarily ideal, so some new golfers are going to prefer to head to a local store instead. When you take this route, you can hold each club you are considering, and the store might even let you hit some shots right then and there (if they have a driving range or hitting net). If you are more of an 'old school' shopper – meaning you like to see and touch items before you buy them – you'll almost certainly find yourself in a local golf store at some point.

- Online is the way to go for used clubs. We are going to talk more about used golf clubs in a minute, but for now, we are just going to say that you'll want to shop online if you are looking to go in the used direction. Many online golf retailers will have a used section, and you can also turn to eBay for a wealth of used clubs. While your local golf shop may happen to have a bin with a few used clubs, it's unlikely they'll have the level of inventory needed to help you assemble a good set. If you do decide to go with used clubs for your first set, the web is going to be your best friend in that pursuit.

- Compare prices. You may think at first that the better prices will be found online, but that isn't always the case. Often, when talking about new clubs at least, the prices will be exactly the same online and in person. And, if you have to pay shipping on the online purchase, you may wind up better off buying from a physical store. Just like when buying anything else, compare prices at various outlets to make sure you are getting a fair deal.

For many people, the process of buying clubs is going to wind up being a blend of online and in-person shopping. You may find some clubs and accessories that you like in person, while you might wind up tracking down the rest over the web. There is no right or wrong here, as long as you are taking the time to consider your options and make sure the price you are paying is fair.

New or Used?

Moving on, let's get into the debate on new vs. used clubs for a beginner. There are certainly pros and cons to each option, so you shouldn't dismiss either one out of hand without a closer look. Quite obviously, the big advantage with new clubs is the fact that well… they are new! You can be sure that the clubs aren't worn out, because you are the first player to put them to use. They will look great when they go into your bag, and you should get a long useful life from them, as well. Also, since you are buying the new models on the market, you stand to enjoy the benefits that come with playing the latest technology the game has to offer. If you were to reach back into golf history by a couple years (or more than a couple), you may be lacking the benefits offered by some of the newest developments.

The downside that comes along with new clubs is, of course, the price. Buying used clubs is almost always going to provide you with a discount as compared to new equipment. The amount of that discount is going to depend on the age of the club in question, its condition, popularity, and more. If you buy a used driver, for example, that is only a year old and has been played very little, you might not save much as compared to a brand-new club. On the other hand, buying a five-year-old driver that has been used for hundreds of rounds is going to mean big savings.

With used clubs, the only motivation to go this direction is the savings we mentioned in the previous paragraph. If the prices

were the same, you'd always buy new, because why not? It's only the cost difference that makes it worthwhile to consider used clubs. So, are the savings worth it? That depends on a number of factors. If you are saving money by purchasing clubs that are near the end of their useful life anyway, you might not actually be saving at all. Those clubs may wear out in the near future, meaning you'll have to pick up new clubs and spend more money. Purchasing used clubs is only a good option when you can find clubs that have enough useful life left to justify the cost savings.

Overall, we would actually recommend that you buy new clubs as opposed to used clubs. Yes, you'll pay a little bit more, but you don't yet have the trained eye required to pick out good used clubs on the market. An experienced golfer will know what to look for in terms of wear and tear on a club, but you don't have that knowledge just yet. Rather than risking buying a used club or used set that doesn't have much life left, stick with new and be sure you are getting something in good condition.

Chapter Eight
Golf Bags and Accessories

So far in this guide, we have talked exclusively about golf clubs. That is an important piece of the puzzle, of course, as you aren't going to be able to play golf without a set of clubs. However, if you head to the course with a set of 14 clubs and nothing more, you aren't going to get very far. There are a number of accessories to consider when stocking up to get started in this game.

The first thing you'll want to think about in this category is a bag which can hold all of your clubs as you make your way around the course. There are tons of bags on the market, of course, so you won't lack for options when shopping. The best way to sort through the variety you'll find is to think about whether you are going to walk or ride in a cart for most of your rounds. If you plan to walk most of the time, look for a lightweight bag with a stand. These types of bags are extremely popular, and some are quite affordable. When shopping, don't go too far in the cheap direction on this purchase. Spending on the money on a quality bag is an investment which will likely pay off over the long run. A good bag is going to have comfortable straps, durable parts (like zippers), and a sturdy stand. There is also room here for a little personal style, so be sure to pick out a color that suits you nicely.

If you don't see much walking of the course in your future, you can feel free to buy a bigger bag. A 'cart bag' is one which is

suited for placing on the back of a power cart. These types of bags are bigger and heavier than carry bags, but that really isn't a problem since you'll only be carrying it from your car to the car. As a result of picking a bigger bag, you can store more stuff inside for your day on the course – things like extra clothes, drinks, snacks, etc. Cart bags do tend to be more expensive than stand bags, so keep that in mind.

Stocking Up

Once you have a bag, your shopping experience is still not over. Let's go through some of the other items you'll want to obtain before making your first tee time.

- Golf balls. Even a total beginner will understand that golf balls are necessary to play this game. You could walk up to the first tee with a bag full of shiny clubs, but if you don't have a ball to place on the tee, you aren't going to be able to play a single shot. As a total beginner, it doesn't particularly matter what kind of golf balls you use. It's certainly not necessary to purchase high-end golf balls, as the premium balls on the market are not going to provide anything that you need at this point, and they may actually make it harder for you to make progress. Low-priced golf balls are where you should be starting, especially since you're likely to lose more than a few along the way in the early days. Just as is the case with golf clubs, you can always choose to upgrade to more expensive golf balls later on down the line as your game progresses.

- Golf shoes. Yes – you should have golf-specific shoes to wear while practicing and while on the course. Plenty of people who are new to the game seem to think they can get away with just wearing tennis shoes, but that isn't a good idea for a number of reasons. For one thing, golf shoes are designed in a way that allows them to provide a stable base while making a golf swing back and through. A standard tennis shoe is not likely to be supportive in the same way. Also, the traction built into the bottom of a golf shoe will help to prevent you from slipping. If you try to make a full swing in tennis shoes, especially on damp grass, you'll find that it's hard to keep your feet under your properly. You don't need to buy the most expensive pair of shoes on the market, but be sure to get a solid pair that will feel comfortable on your feet all day long.

- Golf tees. This is an admittedly small item, but it is a necessity nonetheless. When you pay for a round of golf, you may find that the course offers tees for free, either in the pro shop or on the first tee (or even in the cart, if you are riding). Additionally, it's a good idea to pick up a small package of tees to keep in your bag, just in case the course you are playing does not have any available. As you would expect, golf tees are quite affordable, so this item is not going to take up much of your budget.

- Golf glove. While it is not necessary to play golf with a glove, most players do like the feeling that a glove provides. For a beginner, we recommend playing with a glove because your

hands are not going to be used to the wear and tear that they will experience as you practice or play. Without a glove, it's likely that you would develop blisters in short order (you might develop blisters even with a glove, but they should take a little longer to show up). There is no trick to picking out a golf glove – just try on a few at your local golf shop and pick out the one you like best.

As time goes by, you will inevitably pick up other items related to golf that will find a home in your bag, at least some of the time. For instance, if you wind up with a tee time on a rainy day, you may buy a golf umbrella that you can add to your bag anytime there is rain in the forecast. The same can be said for rain gear like a jacket and some waterproof pants. Also, there is the whole world of distance measuring devices to get into as well, such as laser rangefinders and GPS units. You don't need to worry about those just yet but picking up a distance measuring device at some point may be a good idea if you get serious about the game.

One final note we would like to make in this section relates to the topic of golf attire. Depending on the kinds of courses you are playing, it may be necessary to have golf-specific attire in your wardrobe. Most country clubs have a specific dress code in place, and some higher-end public courses do as well. You don't have to invest thousands of dollars in your clothes or anything like that, but it is smart to pick up at least a few golf-specific pieces so you are ready whenever you get the chance to play.

Chapter Nine
Routine Maintenance

Fortunately, there is not a lot of upkeep required when it comes to your golf equipment. You shouldn't have to spend long hours taking care of your gear just to be ready to head out to the links on the weekend for a round with your friends. With that said, there are some things you can do to both improve the way your equipment performs, and also extend its useful life.

As far as your golf clubs themselves are concerned, the maintenance that you should perform actually starts while you are on the course. After each shot, make it a habit of wiping off the club head before placing the club back in your bag. This is a good habit for a couple of reasons. First, it will ensure that the club is clean for the next time you need to use it during the round. Instead of having to clean up the club before hitting your next shot, you can just take the club from your bag and get down to work. Also, wiping the club off after every shot will help prevent grass and other debris from building up in the grooves. It only takes a moment to wipe off your club as you put it back in the bag – assuming you have a towel close at hand – and doing so will keep your clubs clean and ready to go all round long.

Don't Forget Your Grips

In addition to the club heads, you also need to pay attention to the grips on your clubs. As you use your clubs in practice and on the course, they are likely to get a little oily and slippery. If you

notice this during a round, you can simply take your towel and wipe the grip off for a moment. When your round is over, and you are back home, consider using a wet towel and a little bit of soap (a standard dish soap should work) to clean your grips more thoroughly. Wipe them down with a dry towel after washing and then let them air out before they go back in the bag.

So, keeping your clubs in good working order is easy enough. What about the rest of your equipment? Check out the tips below.

- Golf shoes. The main task here is just to keep your golf shoes relatively clean so they are always ready for your next round. As soon as you are done with a round – after you have walked off the last green, of course – take a moment to clean off your shoes. Specifically, pay attention to the grass that may have built up on the bottom of your shoes as you played. Some courses even have compressed air somewhere near the pro shop or clubhouse that you can use to blow the grass off of your shoes. You also don't want to let your shoe sit around wet for too long after playing a round of golf in the rain, or even on a course that was covered in dew. Do your best to dry your shoes off after you play, and change into some other shoes for the drive home.

- Golf bag. There shouldn't be much cleaning involved with your golf bag unless you happen to drop it in the mud or something. With that said, you may want to go through your bag from time to time just to take out things that don't need

to be in there anymore. If you become a serious golfer and find yourself playing frequently, you may be surprised to see just how quickly random stuff can build up in the bag. Take a moment to review the contents of your bag on occasion to make sure you aren't carrying out things that you don't need.

- Golf glove. The key to getting the longest possible lifespan out of your golf glove is to keep it dry. That being the case, try to take it off after each shot and place it somewhere that it will be allowed to dry out. You might want to stick it partially in your pocket with the fingers sticking out, or you might want to attach it to a part of your bag. When you get ready to hit your next shot, you can put it back on and it should be relatively dry and ready to go. Even with proper care, you probably shouldn't expect to get more than a few rounds out of any given glove.

It's not hard to take care of your golf equipment. As long as you are willing to pay attention to a few details, you can keep your gear in good condition and make sure it is always ready to play the next shot.

Conclusion

We have covered a lot of territory in this guide. As a new golfer, you are probably feeling like there is more information out there than you could ever consume, and that is certainly the case to some degree. The key is to filter out what you don't need and focus in on the pieces of information that can help you move your game in the right direction.

There are some basic themes we would like to recap here before we wrap up the guide and send you on your way to get started in golf. First, remember that there is no need to spend large amounts of money when first getting started. Even if you are excited about the possibility of becoming a golfer, there is no guarantee that you will actually like the game. We hope you will, but don't invest thousands of dollars before you have enough experience to confirm that this game is going to become a regular part of your life. Do your best to build a set of clubs on a relatively modest budget and use the money you save to pay for rounds of golf, buckets of balls at the driving range, and maybe even some lessons.

Another key them we hope you'll take away from this guide is the fact that you should be looking for clubs which are easy to hit. If you watch golf on TV, you might be tempted to build a set that looks just like the set used by your favorite professional golfer. That would be a mistake. The pros you see on TV are the best of the best, and you are not yet at a skill level sufficient to use those clubs. That's not to say you won't be at that level someday, but that day is not today. Build a set based on your

current skill level and don't make this game any harder than it needs to be.

Finally, we want to make a point that actually has nothing at all to do with golf equipment. Quite simply, we want to encourage you to have fun out there. Golf is a hard game, and you are going to struggle at first. Don't let those struggles get you down or discourage you from continuing to play. Instead, look at your struggles as a rite of passage. If you stick with it and start to make progress, you will feel a tremendous sense of pride when you see how far you've come.

Thank you for taking the time to read this guide, and we hope you now have an improved understanding of how to build a great beginner set of golf clubs. Happy shopping and we hope to see you on the links!

If you enjoyed this book as much as I've enjoyed writing it, you can subscribe* to my email list for exclusive content and sneak peaks of my future books.

Go to the link below:

http://eepurl.com/dvdC_X

OR

Use the QR Code:

(*Must be 13 years or older to subscribe)

MW00887829